Essential Science ✔

Earth, Moon & Sun

Peter Riley

W
FRANKLIN WATTS
LONDON • SYDNEY

First published in 2006 by Franklin Watts
338 Euston Road, London NW1 3BH

Franklin Watts Australia
Hachette Children's Books
Level 17/207 Kent Street, Sydney NSW 2000

Editor: Rachel Tonkin
Designer: Proof Books
Picture researcher: Diana Morris
Illustrations: Ian Thompson

Picture credits:
Macduff Everton/Corbis: 11; Nick Gundeson/Corbis: 17;
Imagestate/Alamy: cover l; Frank Krahmer/zefa/Corbis: 18;
Werner A. Miller/Corbis: 25; NASA: cover br, 3t, 6, 7l, 7r, 8t, 8b,
13, 26, 27, 28cl; Picturepoint/Topham: cover tr; Roger
Ressmeyer/Corbis: 4bl; Guenter Rossenbach/Corbis: 4tr;
Robin Scagell/SPL: 9; Raoul Slater/WWI/Still Pictures: cover cr;
Tom Walker/Getty Images: 21; Ron Watts/Corbis: 12, 28br.

All other images: Andy Crawford

With thanks to our model Liam Cheung

A CIP catalogue record for this book
is available from the British Library

ISBN-10: 0 7496 6447 9
ISBN-13: 978 0 7496 6447 3

Dewey Classification: 523

Printed in China

CONTENTS

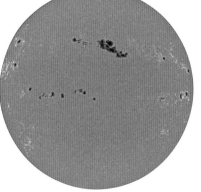

EARTH, MOON AND SUN

Today most people know that the Earth, Moon and Sun are almost spherical (shaped like a ball) but in the past people had other ideas.

As ships go over the horizon, their hulls disappear first.

The flat Earth

People used to think that the Earth was flat. They thought that you just went across its surface covered with hills, valleys, plains and seas until you came to the edge. However, if you watch a ship sailing away it does not get smaller and smaller as it would if the Earth was flat. It disappears in a certain order. The hull disappears, then the cabins above the hull, then the funnels and finally the masts. This suggests that the Earth is curved and could be spherical.

You can see the constellation called Orion which has three stars in a row.

The stars provide a clue

Ancient people grouped stars together into constellations so they could recognise different parts of the sky. If the Earth was flat, the same constellations should appear in the sky wherever you went. When people travelled far to the North or South they found that some constellations disappeared over the horizon and new ones appeared over the opposite horizon. This also suggested that the Earth is curved and could be spherical.

Final proof

When spacecraft, such as satellites, were launched just over 40 years ago, they carried cameras and sent back pictures of the Earth. The pictures showed that the Earth was almost spherical.

The Sun and the Moon

The Sun appears as a circular shape all the time, which suggests that it is spherical. You must never look at the Sun because it is so bright that it can blind you. The Moon sometimes appears circular which suggests that it is also spherical. The other shapes of the Moon, called phases, are due to the way sunlight shines on it.

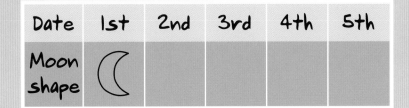

The shape of the moon we see is made by the Sun shining on it, like this torch on a tennis ball.

Data

When scientists do experiments, they make observations and take measurements and record them. This information is called data. It may be in the form of a table, bar chart or line graph. Collect some data about the Moon by trying this activity.

Date	1st	2nd	3rd	4th	5th
Moon shape	🌙				

Prepare a table like the one shown here. Try and look at the Moon each night and draw its shape in the boxes. How does your data compare?

You will find data on many pages in this book. Can you answer the questions on it?

THE SOLAR SYSTEM

Where are the Earth, Moon and Sun in space?
What is a galaxy and what is the difference
between a planet and a moon?

What is the Solar System?

The Solar System is made up of the Sun, the planets and other bodies that orbit the Sun, including moons, asteroids and comets. The Sun is a star. Other stars also have planets and moons orbiting around them.

The planets

There are nine planets in the Solar System. They are divided into five small rocky planets and four large planets which are mostly composed of gas and are called gas giants. The rocky planets are: Mercury, Venus, Earth, Mars and Pluto. The gas giants are: Jupiter, Saturn, Uranus and Neptune.

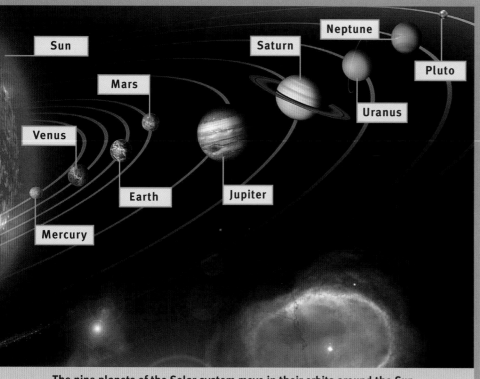

The nine planets of the Solar system move in their orbits around the Sun.

Orbits

An orbit is the path a planet travels around a star. It is also the path of a moon around a planet. The word orbit can be used to describe the movement of a planet. For example, the Earth orbits the Sun once a year.

Planets and moons

A large space object which moves around a star is called a planet. A smaller space object which moves around a planet is called a moon. There may be many planets moving around a star and many moons moving around a planet.

Comets

A comet is a lump of rock and ice that has an orbit that takes it close to the Sun and then far away beyond Pluto. As a comet moves close to the Sun some of the ice melts and forms a long cloudy tail.

A comet's tail points away from the Sun.

Galaxies

If you could travel through the Universe you would see huge groups of millions of stars. They are called galaxies. Some galaxies are like clouds and do not have a special shape. Other galaxies are elliptical or spiral in shape. The Sun is a star in a spiral galaxy called the Milky Way.

The Solar System is in a spiral galaxy called the Milky Way.

Asteroids

There is a huge number of rocks which form a ring between the orbits of Mars and Jupiter. The rocks are called asteroids and the ring is called the asteroid belt.

Planet distance

1 Is the orbit of Mars nearer to Earth's orbit than the orbit of Venus?

2 How much faster than Mars does Mercury travel?

3 How does the speed of planets change as they get further away from the Sun?

Planet	Distance to Sun (millions km)	Speed in orbit km/s
Mercury	58	48
Venus	108	35
Earth	150	30
Mars	228	24

THE STARS AND THE SUN

The Sun is a star but where do stars come from and how do they form?

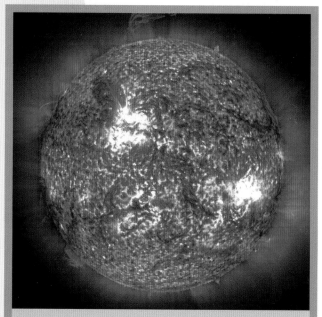

The Sun gives out huge amounts of light and heat. Note the solar flare near the top (see opposite).

The Big Bang

Scientists believe an explosion, called the Big Bang, created the universe about 13 billion years ago. It created new substances – two gases called hydrogen and helium. Stars most likely began as clouds of hydrogen and dust. The force of gravity pulled the clouds together to form thicker and thicker clumps. These formed young stars which began to heat up. Once a star reaches a certain temperature, the hydrogen in it begins to burn and releases light. This lasts for billions of years until the hydrogen is used up.

Old stars to new

When a star has only a small amount of hydrogen remaining it may fade away and release large amounts of dust, or it may explode and form a supernova. The gases and dust that are released spread out through space and make clouds in which more stars form. The Sun formed in a gas cloud five billion years ago.

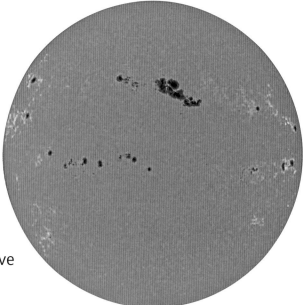

The Sun has spots on its surface (see opposite).

Spots and flares

It is 4,000 °C on the Sun's surface. There is a great churning of substances inside the Sun which make parts of it behave like a magnet. The pull of magnetic forces makes dark patches of cooler gas on the surface called sun spots. The churning of substances also shoots out huge clouds of gas called solar flares.

The spinning Sun

If the Sun is viewed everyday through a telescope as shown in the picture, the sunspots move. They show that the Sun is slowly turning. It takes 30 days for the Sun to turn round once.

The Sun can be studied by focusing a picture of it on a screen using a special type of telescope.

How near are the stars?

The distance of stars from Earth is measured in light years. A light year is the distance travelled by a ray of light in one year (9.5 million, million kilometres). Here are the distances of some stars from Earth.

1 Which one is the nearest?

2 Which one is the furthest?

3 Think of the light reaching Earth from Polaris tonight. In which year did it leave the star?

4 In which year were you born? When did light reaching Earth in that year from Betelgeuse begin its journey?

Star	Distance in light years
Polaris	6
Deneb	1,006
Regulus	84
Arcturus	36
Betelgeuse	520

THE EARTH AND GRAVITY

**The Earth is a huge ball of rock in space.
The pull of gravity moves the Earth around
the Sun, and the Moon around the Earth.**

How the Earth formed

The Earth and the other planets formed from a spinning disc of gas
and dust around the Sun. The spinning of the disc gave the planets
their spins and the energy to move through space.

Gravity between the Sun and the Earth

There is a force of gravity between any two objects in the universe.
The Sun's force of gravity pulls on the Earth as it tries to move in a
straight line through space. The force of the Sun pulls the Earth
towards it so that the Earth follows an elliptical path around the
Sun called an orbit. The Sun's gravity pulls on the other planets in
the Solar System and makes them
travel round in orbits, too.
The force of gravity of the
planets pull on the Sun
and make it wobble
slightly as it spins.

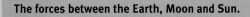
The forces between the Earth, Moon and Sun.

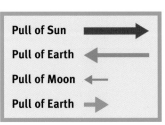

Pull of Sun	→
Pull of Earth	←
Pull of Moon	←
Pull of Earth	→

Gravity between the Earth and the Moon

As the Moon tries to move out into space, the pull from the Earth's gravity is just strong enough to keep pulling the Moon back towards the Earth. This makes the Moon travel round the Earth in an orbit. The Moon's gravity is weaker than the Earth's. Its pull on the Earth makes the surface of the oceans and seas rise and fall.

The Moon's gravity makes tides rise and fall on the shore.

Changing weight

Weight is due to the pull of Earth's gravity on the mass of an object. The table shows how the weight of a mass changes as it moved away from the Earth.

1 By how much has the weight changed as it has gone into space?
2 Does the pull of gravity get stronger, weaker or stay the same as an object moves away from the Earth?
3 What do you think would happen to the object's weight as it moved further from the Earth?

Mass (kg)	Weight (N) on Earth's surface	Weight (N) 15,000 km in space
1	10	2

THE MOON

The Moon is our nearest neighbour in space. It may have formed from a massive crash between planets. If you could visit it you would find it a silent world of rocks and dust.

The Big Whack

Nobody is sure how the Moon formed, but many scientists believe that about 4.5 billion years ago the Earth was struck by a planet roughly the size of Mars. The crash, called the Big Whack, produced great heat, which melted the planet then turned some of it into vapour that rushed out into space. The vapour cooled as it moved away and formed a ring of rocky lumps around the Earth. In time, these lumps of rock crashed together to form the Moon.

The Moon does not just appear in the night sky but also appears in the daytime sky too.

If you were to visit the Moon you would find that much of it is covered in dust. The footprints you left behind would last for millions of years as there is no atmosphere to blow the dust around. As there are no gases to carry sound, like the air on Earth, you would find that the Moon is a silent place.

Astronauts collected rock samples from the Moon that have helped scientists to understand how the Moon may have formed.

On the Moon's surface

If you look at a full Moon you can see that part of its surface is white and part of it is grey. The white parts are formed by mountains and the grey parts are formed by plains covered in lava which cooled and turned to a solid long ago. When you look at the Moon with binoculars or a small telescope you can see circles on the surface. These are craters made by asteroids which crashed into its surface millions of years ago.

Planets and their moons

Here are the planets in the Solar System which have moons.

1 Two planets do not have any moons. Look at the picture of the Solar System on page 6 and this table to find out which ones they are.
2 How does the number of moons around each planet change as you move outwards from the Earth to Pluto?

Planet	number of moons
Earth	1
Mars	2
Jupiter	28
Saturn	30
Uranus	21
Neptune	8
Pluto	1

SUN, MOON AND EARTH

The Sun, Moon and Earth are the three objects in space that everyone knows. How big are they, what are the distances between them and why do the Moon and Sun seem the same size?

How big are they?

The Sun has a diameter of 1, 392,000 km.

The Moon has a diameter of 3, 476 km.

The Earth has a diameter of 12, 756 km.

If you think of the Sun as the size of a beach ball, the Earth the size of a pea and the Moon the size of a tiny bead you can get some idea of how their sizes compare.

How far away is the Moon?

The Moon is 384, 500 km from the Earth.

How far away is the Sun?

The Sun is about 149, 600, 000 kilometres from the Earth.

The effect of distance

The Sun and the Moon appear to be about the same size in the sky. This is due to the Moon being very close to the Earth and the Sun being a long way away. The short distance of the small Moon from the Earth makes it appear large. The long distance of the huge Sun from the Earth makes it appear small.

When the beach ball is moved into the distance it appears smaller than it really is.

An eclipse of the Sun

As the Moon travels in orbit around the Earth, it sometimes passes directly between the Sun and the Earth. When this happens an eclipse of the Sun occurs and the light of the Sun is blotted out by the Moon moving in front of it.

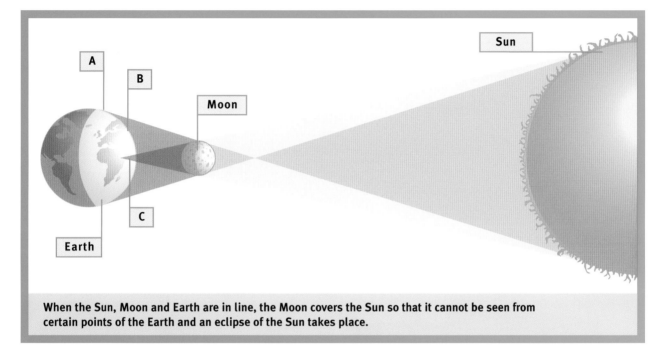

When the Sun, Moon and Earth are in line, the Moon covers the Sun so that it cannot be seen from certain points of the Earth and an eclipse of the Sun takes place.

An eclipse of the Moon

Sometimes the Earth passes directly between the Sun and the Moon and stops the Sun's light reaching the Moon. When this happens an eclipse of the Moon occurs and a shadow of the Earth is cast on its surface. The light from the Sun is blotted out by the Earth.

Where on Earth does an eclipse of the Sun occur?

An total eclipse does not occur on all parts of the Earth – just where the Moon's shadow, the umbra, is darkest. In the paler shadow, called the penumbra, a partial eclipse is seen.

Look at the diagram above and see if you can work out the answers to the questions.

1 Where will a total eclipse occur?
2 Where will a partial eclipse occur?
3 In which place will an eclipse not occur?

THE SPINNING EARTH

**The Earth spins round in space
and this gives us day and night.**

Rotation

The spinning movement is also called rotation. The Earth rotates around its axis. This is an imaginary line that runs from the North Pole, through the centre of the Earth to the South Pole. If you were in a space ship looking down on the North Pole you would see that the Earth rotates in an anticlockwise direction.

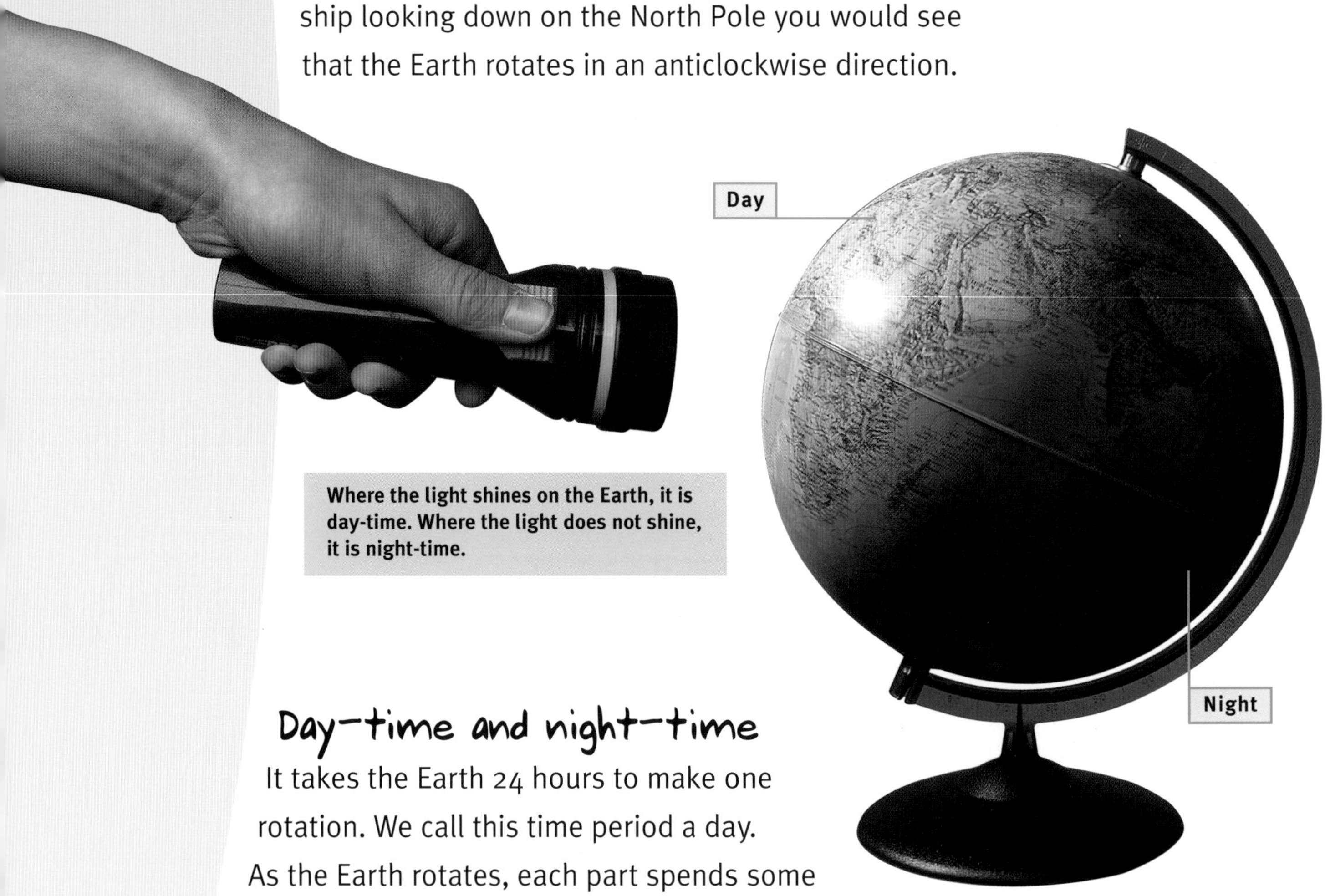

Day

Where the light shines on the Earth, it is day-time. Where the light does not shine, it is night-time.

Night

Day-time and night-time

It takes the Earth 24 hours to make one rotation. We call this time period a day. As the Earth rotates, each part spends some time facing towards the Sun (day-time) and some time facing away from it (night-time).

The tilting Earth

The axis of the Earth is tilted at 23.5 degrees from a vertical line running through the centre of the Earth. The Earth always tilts in the same direction as it goes round the Sun (see page 22).

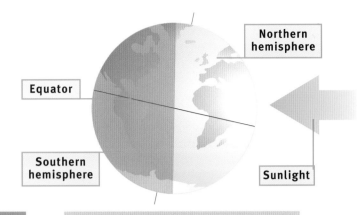

Northern hemisphere

Equator

Southern hemisphere

Sunlight

The tilt of the Earth means that some parts of the Earth are tipped towards the light and some parts are tipped away from it.

This city is in a hemisphere tilted away from the Sun so it starts to go dark early.

WESTLAKE CENTER

Hemispheres

There is an imaginary line around the Earth called the Equator. The region above it is called the Northern hemisphere and the region below it is called the Southern hemisphere. When a hemisphere is tilted towards the Sun, the places in it receive more than 12 hours of daylight. When it is tilted away from the Sun, the places receive fewer than 12 hours daylight.

Times to spin

All planets spin round. Here are the times for some of the planets to spin round:

1 Which planets have longer days than the Earth?
2 Look at the picture of the planets on page 6 to help you work out which planets have the shorter days – small planets or large planets?

Planet	Length of spin
Mercury	58.7 days
Venus	243 days
Mars	24 hrs, 37 mins
Jupiter	9 hrs, 55 mins
Saturn	10 hrs, 39 mins
Uranus	17 hrs, 14 mins
Neptune	16 hrs, 7 mins
Pluto	6 days, 9 hrs

THE PATH OF THE SUN

The Sun appears to follow a path across the sky.

The Sun rises over the eastern horizon at dawn and disappears over the western horizon at sunset.

The horizon

The horizon is the place where the sky appears to meet the Earth. If you are at the coast the horizon is where the sky seems to meet the surface of the sea. If you are inland it can be the place where the sky meets hilltops, trees or the roofs of buildings. During the day, the Sun appears to move across the sky. This is not caused by the Sun moving but by the Earth turning on its axis.

Using shadows

We cannot look directly at the Sun as it can blind us. But we can use a shadow stick and look at the shadows it casts in the sunlight. A shadow is made when light strikes an opaque object. When a shadow forms, it points in the opposite direction to the Sun. If a compass is used with a shadow stick, the direction in which the shadow points can be used to find the direction of the Sun. For example, if the shadow points west then the Sun is in the east.

The length of the shadow can be used to find the height of the Sun in the sky. For example, when the shadow is long the Sun is low in the sky and when the shadow is short the Sun is high in the sky.

A shadow stick can be used to find how the position of the Sun changes during the day.

The Sun follows a curved path across the sky.

Where is the Sun?

The table shows the direction and length of shadows cast by a shadow stick.

Time	Shadow direction	Shadow length (cm)
6.00 am	west	100
9.00 am	north west	75
Noon	north	50
3.00 pm	north east	75
6.00 pm	east	100

1 In which part of the sky is the Sun at each of the five times shown in the table?
2 How does the shadow length change during the day?
3 When is the Sun highest in the sky?
4 When is the Sun lowest in the sky?

THE SUN'S CHANGING PATH

The height and length of the Sun's path across the sky changes during the year.

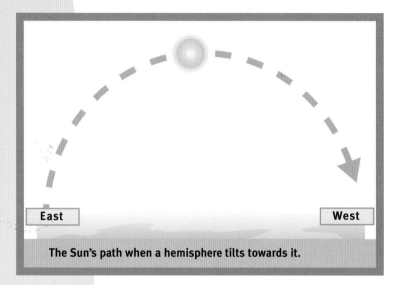

The Sun's path when a hemisphere tilts towards it.

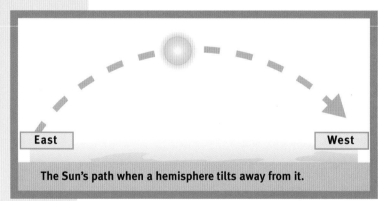

The Sun's path when a hemisphere tilts away from it.

High in the sky

When a hemisphere (see page 17) is tilted towards the Sun, the sunrise occurs further to the east along the horizon, the Sun rises high in the sky and sets further to the west. It spends a long time in the sky and the days are long.

Low in the sky

When a hemisphere is tilted away from the Sun, the sunrise occurs further to the west, the Sun does not rise as high in the sky and sets further towards the east. It spends a much shorter time in the sky and the days are short.

Long and short days

The tilt of the Earth is the main cause of the different seasons (see page 22). It also means that the length of days and nights vary at different times of the year, depending on where a place is in realation to the equator. Days get longer or shorter according to the season and the proximity to the poles.

The midnight sun

When the North Pole or South Pole is tilted towards the Sun, the places nearby receive sunlight for 24 hours each day – even at midnight. The Sun does not set. It just dips low towards the horizon then rises again.

The darkest days

When the North Pole or South Pole is tilted away from the Sun, the places nearby do not receive any sunlight. The sun does not rise in the sky and places have 24 hours of darkness each day.

This picture was taken with a camera that can take an image over 24 hours. It shows the path of the Sun over 24 hours at a pole when it is tilted towards the Sun.

How times change

Here are the times for sunrise and sunset for a place for one day for each month of the year in a place in the Northern hemisphere.

1 Make a graph of the data by having the time on the horizontal x axis from 1 am to 12 midnight and the months on the vertical y axis.
2 How do the sunrise and sunset times change?
3 How does the day length change each month?
4 What do you predict will happen to the day length in the rest of the year?

Month	Sunrise	Sunset
January	8.00 am	4.30 pm
February	7.30 am	5.00 pm
March	6.00 am	6.00 pm
April	5.30 am	7.30 pm
May	5.00 am	8.30 pm
June	4.30 am	10.00 pm
July	5.00 am	8.30 pm

A YEAR ON EARTH

It takes a year for the Earth to travel round the Sun. In many places the year is divided into four seasons.

Years and leap years

The Earth takes 365.25 rotations or days to travel round the Sun. This period of time is called a year.

As the number of days is not exact, people have made most years into 365 days but every fourth year has 366 days and is called a leap year.

The seasons

Winter

When a hemisphere is tilted away from the Sun, it is winter. The Sun does not spend a long time in the sky (see page 20) and so it gives little heat to the Earth's surface and the weather is cold. There is one day that has a shorter period of daylight than any other day. This is called the winter solstice.

Spring

In spring, the hemisphere is neither tilting towards or away from the Sun. The path of the Sun has become longer than in winter and more heat reaches the Earth's surface. There is one day that has the same number of hours of daylight and darkness. This day is called the spring equinox.

Summer

When a hemisphere is tilted towards the Sun, it is summer. The Sun spends a long time in the sky and gives a great deal of heat to the Earth's surface and the weather is hot. There is one day that has a longer period of daylight than any other day of the year. This is the summer solstice.

Autumn

In autumn, the hemisphere is neither tilting towards or away from the Sun. The path of the Sun has become shorter in the sky than in summer and less heat reaches the Earth's surface. There is one day that has the same number of hours of daylight and darkness. This day is called the autumn equinox.

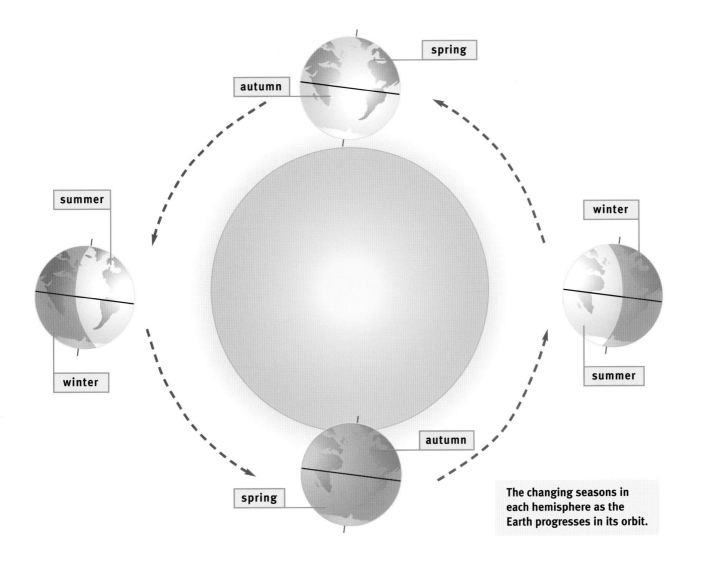

spring

autumn

summer

winter

winter

summer

autumn

spring

The changing seasons in each hemisphere as the Earth progresses in its orbit.

Opposite seasons

While the Northern hemisphere has winter, spring, summer and autumn, the Southern hemisphere has the opposite – summer, autumn, winter and spring. This is due to the Southern hemisphere tilting in the opposite direction to the Northern hemisphere.

How far does the Earth travel?

The Earth travels in its orbit at a speed of about 10, 400 km per hour.

1 How far does it travel in 10 hours?

2 How far does it travel in 24 hours?

3 How far does it travel in 1 minute?

THE MOON IN ITS ORBIT

The Moon moves in a path around the Earth. As it travels, different amounts of its surface are lit by the Sun and make it seem to change shape.

The Moon's orbit

The Moon moves in an anticlockwise orbit round the Earth as the Earth moves around the Sun. It takes the Moon 29.5 days to travel round the Earth. The orbit of the Moon is not in line with the orbit of the Earth around the Sun. If it was, the Moon would come between the Sun and the Earth at each new Moon and cause an eclipse (see page 15). The Moon spins as it moves in its orbit. The speed at which it spins keeps the same side always facing the Earth.

The phases of the Moon

The Moon does not produce light like the Sun. It shines by the sunlight that is reflected from its surface. The area of the Moon that we can see from the Earth which reflects light changes as the Moon moves in its orbit. These different areas are known as phases. They occur in order each month as the diagram shows.

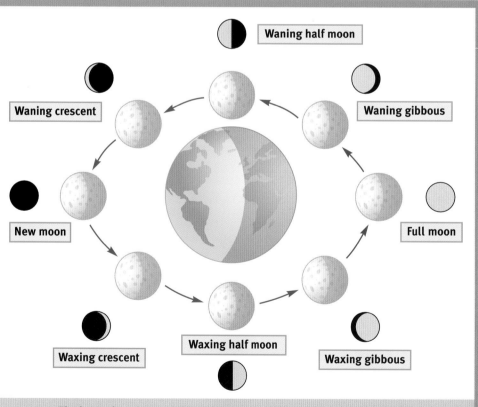

Waning half moon

Waning crescent

Waning gibbous

New moon

Full moon

Waxing crescent

Waxing half moon

Waxing gibbous

The inner ring shows eight positions of the Moon as it orbits the Earth.
The outer ring shows how the Moon looks from the Earth at each position.

The Moon forms a crescent when it is waxing and waning.

The new Moon

At each new Moon, the Moon is a little above or below the Sun in the sky and an eclipse of the Sun does not occur.

At this time, the surface of the Moon facing the Earth is in complete darkness and cannot be seen. After a day, a crescent of light is seen on the Moon's surface and this is what most people call the new Moon.

Waxing and waning

The Moon is said to be waxing when the size of its shining surface increases each night. The Moon is said to be waning when the size of its shining surface decreases each night.

Phases

1 What are the three phases of the Moon shown here.
2 In what order do they occur after a new Moon as the Moon travels in its orbit.

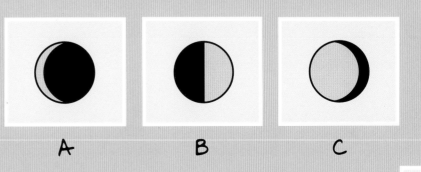

A   B   C

EXPLORING SPACE

People who lived long ago made many discoveries about space simply by looking at the sky and noticing changes over time. Today we have many kinds of equipment to help us find out more.

Rocket engines fire to lift this spacecraft into the sky.

Early discoveries

People's early discoveries of space were based on observation with the naked eye. They could see and record the path of the Sun, the phases of the Moon and the position of the stars, which did not move, and the planets, which did move (planet means wanderer). They explained these things in various ways (see panel) but some people began to question these ideas. In particular, the invention of the telescope allowed astronomers to study the skies in even more detail. Slowly, people's ideas about space began to change.

The rocket engine

More powerful telescopes were developed but the invention of the rocket engine led to the development of spacecraft. The rocket engine is powerful enough to push a spacecraft away from the pull of the Earth's gravity.

Humans in space

Some spacecraft carry humans. The spacecraft may take astronauts to and from space, like the space shuttle. There are also space stations in which humans live that orbit the Earth. The people living in space stations study the effects of living in space. The results of their investigations will help design spacecraft to visit other planets, such as Mars.

Space probes

Probes carry instruments to measure the conditions in space and cameras to take photographs. Some probes that land on other planets or moons carry vehicles which can travel over their surfaces and examine rocks and measure the conditions in the environment.

This vehicle travelled over the surface of Mars and carried equipment to investigate the conditions there.

Early discoveries

For a long time people believed that the Earth was the centre of the Universe and everything moved round it attached to a series of solid crystal spheres. They believed that comets were clouds in the air.

Tycho Brahe (1546–1601) studied a comet with the naked eye. He found it was further away than the Moon and appeared to move through space.

Galileo (1564–1642) built a telescope to see further into space. He discovered moons moving round Jupiter.

Johannes Kepler (1571–1630) made studies on how planets, including the Earth, moved and found they moved in elliptical orbits round the Sun.

1 What early beliefs did Tycho Brahe show to be wrong?

2 Why were people surprised by Galileo's observations on the moons?

3 Why do you think people did not like Kepler's discovery?

CAN YOU REMEMBER THE ESSENTIALS?

Here are the essential science facts about the Earth, Moon and Sun. They are set out in the order you can read about them in the book. Spend a couple of minutes learning each set of facts. If you can learn them all, you know all the essentials about the Earth, Moon and Sun.

The Solar System (pages 6-7)

The Solar System is made up of the Sun and the nine planets which revolve around it.
A planet moves round the Sun. A moon moves round a planet. An orbit is a path taken by a planet or moon in space.

The Earth and gravity (pages 10-11)

The Earth formed from a disc of gas and dust.
The Sun's gravity pulls the Earth round in its orbit.
The Earth's gravity pulls the Moon round it in an orbit.

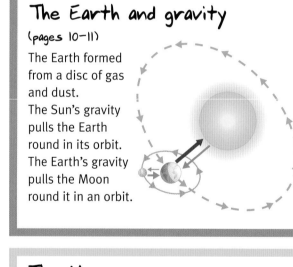

The stars and the Sun (pages 8-9)

It is believed that the Universe began with an explosion called the Big Bang.
The Sun is made from two gases – hydrogen and helium.
There are spots and flares on the surface of the Sun.
The Sun rotates once in thirty days.

The Moon (pages 12-13)

The Moon may have formed when two planets crashed together.
The white parts of the Moon are mountains.
The grey parts of the Moon are plains.
The circles you can see on the Moon are called craters.
The Moon does not have an atmosphere.

Sun, Moon and Earth
(pages 14-15)

The Sun is much larger than the Earth and the Moon.
The Sun is much further away from the Earth than the Moon.
The great distance between the Sun and Moon make the Sun appear to be the same size as the Moon.
An eclipse of the Sun occurs when the Moon passes between the Sun and the Earth.

A year on Earth (pages 22-23)

It takes the Earth a year to travel round the Sun.
In many places the year is divided into four seasons.
The shortest period of daylight occurs at the winter solstice.
The longest period of daylight occurs at the summer solstice.
A day at which the length of day and night is the same is called an equinox.

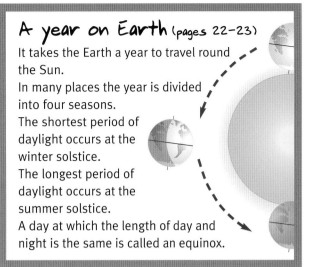

The spinning Earth (pages 18-19)

The Earth rotates around its axis.
It takes the Earth a day to make one rotation.
The axis of the Earth is tilted.
The tilt affects the length of day and night at a place on the Earth's surface.

The Moon in its orbit
(pages 24-25)

The Moon moves in an orbit around the Earth.
It takes the Moon almost a month to complete one orbit.
The Moon rotates but keeps the same side facing the Earth.
The area of light from the Sun reflected from the Moon is called a phase.
The phases of the Moon change as it moves round its orbit.

The path of the Sun
(pages 16-17)

The Sun appears over the eastern horizon at dawn.
The Sun rises in the sky in the morning.
The Sun sinks in the sky in the afternoon.
The Sun disappears over the western horizon at sunset.
The length and position of shadows can be used to find the movement of the Sun in the sky.

The Sun's changing path
(pages 20-21)

When a hemisphere is tilted towards the Sun, the Sun makes a long, high path in the sky.
When a hemisphere is tilted away from the Sun, the Sun makes a short, low path in the sky.
When a pole is tilted towards the Sun, the Sun does not set in the sky.
When a pole is tilted away from the Sun, the Sun does not rise in the sky.

Exploring space (pages 26-27)

Early people made observations on space simply by looking at the sky.
The telescope allows more objects in space to be seen.
Rocket engines are used to launch spacecraft.
Space probes carry equipment to investigate space and the objects in it.
Humans can investigate space from space stations in orbit around the Earth.

GLOSSARY

Asteroid A small planet.

Astronaut A person who is specially trained to live and work in space.

Atmosphere The mixture of gases that surrounds a planet or moon.

Axis An imaginary line running through the centre of the Earth from the North to the South Pole.

Comet A large lump of rock and ice in orbit round the Sun.

Constellation A group of stars that were named by ancient peoples to map out the night skies.

Energy Something which allows an object or a living thing to take part in an activity, such as moving or giving out light.

Elliptical A line which is oval in shape.

Equinox A time of year when day and night are the same length of time.

Galaxy A huge group of stars in space.

Gravity A force of attraction which exists between any two objects in the universe but only causes movement when one object is very much larger than the other.

Hemisphere Either the northern or southern half of the Earth.

Moon The large object in orbit round the Earth. It can also refer to any object in orbit around a planet.

North and South Pole The points on the Earth's surface at each end of the Earth's axis.

Opaque Something that you cannot see through.

Orbit The path taken by a planet around a star or a moon around a planet.

Planet A large object which is in orbit around a star.

Probe An unmanned space vehicle, carrying scientific instruments, which is sent from Earth to explore space.

Rocket engine An engine which shoots out a jet of hot gases to produce a force to move a spacecraft.

Rotation The moving of an object around its centre, such as the moving of the Earth around its axis.

Solar flare Clouds of gas which shoot out from the Sun.

Star A huge ball of gas made from hydrogen and helium.

Solstice The time when the Sun either rises to its highest point in the sky or sinks to its lowest point in the sky.

Space station A space vehicle in which astronauts can live and work.

Sun spot A patch of cool gas on the Sun's surface.

Supernova A massive star that suddenly increases in brightness and releases a huge amount of energy. This happens because the inside of the star collapses and triggers a violent explosion.

Universe All of space and everything that is in it.

Weight The force of an object pressing down towards the centre of the Earth as a result of gravity.

ANSWERS

The Solar System (pages 6–7)

1 No.
2 Twice as fast.
3 It decreases.

The stars and the Sun (pages 8–9)

1 Polaris.
2 Deneb.
3 Six years before the date you saw the star.
4 520 years before the year you were born.

The Earth and gravity (pages 10–11)

1 It has decreased by 8 N.
2 Gets weaker.
3 It would get smaller.

The Moon (pages 12–13)

1 Mercury, Venus.
2 It increases to a maximum at Saturn and then decreases again.

Sun, Moon and Earth (pages 14–15)

1 C
2 B
3 A

The spinning Earth (pages 16–17)

1 Mercury, Venus, Mars, Pluto.
2 Large planets.

The path of the Sun (pages 18–19)

1 6.00 am — low in the east; 9.00 am — higher in the south east; noon — high in the south; 3.00 pm lower in the south west; 6.00 pm — low in the west.

2 It decreases in the morning and increases in the afternoon.
3 At noon.
4 At 6.00 am and 6.00 pm

The Sun's changing path (pages 20–21)

2 Sunrise times get earlier until June then get later again. Sunset times get later until June then get earlier again.
3 It increases from January to June then decreases from June to July.
4 It will decrease.

A year on Earth (pages 22–23)

1 104, 000 km.
2 249, 600 km.
3 173.3 km.

The Moon in its orbit (pages 24–25)

1 A = waning crescent; B = waxing half moon; C = waning gibbous.
2 B, C, A.

Exploring space (pages 26–27)

1 Comets were not clouds but were out in space. Objects in space did not move in crystal spheres.
2 They thought everything moved around the Earth.
3 It meant that the Earth was no longer the centre of the universe. It was less important.

INDEX